UNDERSTANDING CONVERSION

a cautionary prophetic declaration for born-again believers

Written by:

GARY WAYNE LONES

ISBN 978-1-387-62504-8

All scripture taken from the King James Version Bible (KJV).

To Contact the Author:
VICTORY LIFE CENTER, INC.
PO BOX 445 LORIS, SC. 29569 | 854.213.9841
bishopgarywlones@gmail.com

DEDICATION

This book is dedicated to Carrie L. Lones, my wife, best friend, lifelong companion, and business partner for more than 20 years. She is my soulmate. Through wealth and poverty, hardship and ease, good times and bad, ups and downs, ins and outs, unders and overs, you have remained by my side. You are a priceless gift from God and a woman of virtue in every way!

I want to express my gratitude for the unceasing, unconditional, and selfless love and grace you have shown me over the course of these 21 wonderful years. Your support, tenacity, and dedication have given me the motivation I need to improve as a man in every facet of my life.

The Best is yet to come and I am looking forward to realizing the vision the Lord has placed in our hearts.

FOREWORD

I finished reading your book, and it was wonderful! I adore how you interpreted your points in each section by quoting scripture. For the body of Christ to comprehend salvation, discipleship, and ultimately how to maintain the faith by applying the scriptures to our daily lives, this is unquestionably a necessity! Awesome job brother!

- Dr. Timothy Colisino

INTRODUCTION

For those who do not know me or my background, I have spiritually come from humble beginnings. I was forced to dress up in my mauve-colored Captain Kangaroo suit, complete with my uncomfortable yet fashionable spectator dress shoes, go to church, sit in the most uncomfortable worn-out red velvet pew, and listen to the most uninteresting minister this medieval mediocre church had to offer while helplessly nodding off and slipping into an uncontrollable spiritual coma.

"DEAR GOD, KILL ME PLEASE!" I used to scream to myself as my thoughts would occasionally wander from the endlessly boring sermon to something more interesting and significant, like obnoxiously counting the number of polished brass pipes on the massive organ, the small and speckled squares on the enormously large ceiling, and all the other unresponsive congregation members barely hanging onto life to pass the time. Yes! I would have preferred to die than endure another second of listening. “Church should not be this boring!” I repeatedly practiced in my head.

The Lord, mercifully, saved me in the late 1980s. My way of thinking was completely altered by the preacher the Lord guided me to. It doesn't matter who the preacher or the church was because my point still stands. The first time I heard God's anointed word, it lit a fire inside of me to want to learn more and more.

What was the first verse of Scripture that would determine the direction of my spiritual calling?

“Jesus answered and said unto him, Verily, verily, I say unto thee,

Except a man be born again, he cannot see the kingdom of God." (John 3:3)

Yes, unless I am born-again, how can I comprehend the Kingdom of God?

What was the second verse that would put this calling in its proper perspective?

"Jesus answered, Verily, verily, I say unto thee, Except a man be born of water and of the Spirit, he cannot enter into the kingdom of God." (John 3:5)

That's right! The preacher explained to me from God's word that I could not be saved unless I obeyed the Bible. He sent me home with a ton of verses that explained HOW to be "born of the water," and I gladly followed his instructions. In April of 1989, I repented of my sins and was Baptized in the name of Jesus for the remission of those sins! But now I had to experience spiritual birth. But How?

I have therefore committed my life to studying, praying, fasting, and worship for the next five months. God gave me the gift of His Holy Spirit on September 10, 1989, during an incredible anointed service, and I was given the biblically-required evidence of speaking in tongues. (Acts 2:1-4)

Then, God made it clear to me that I had to experience a new birth in order to KNOW who Jesus truly is. I have gained knowledge and spiritual maturity since that point. I've discovered that discipleship MUST follow your new birth!

Currently, my wife and I have the honor and privilege of leading one of Loris, South Carolina's Best Churches as Senior Pastors! It is a church full of hungry souls who love the Lord and work hard to bring in new believers. For upcoming Kingdom work, our ministry focuses on deliverance, discipleship, and ministerial training.

The anointing makes all the difference, so obey the scriptures and you too can live a dynamic fruitful peaceful life!

Table of Contents

Christianity: Fact or Fiction? 9

1) We MUST Believe 10
2) We MUST be Discipled 11
3) We MUST Suffer 13
4) We MUST Witness 15

What is the SIN CYCLE? 17

SIN CYCLE Chart 18
- Thoughts 19
- Temptation 21
- Transgression 22
- Guilt 23
- Sorry 25

CONVERSION CYCLE 26
- Acknowledgement 27
- Submit To God 28
- Disassociation 30
- Preventative Measure 31
- Conversion 33

CERTIFICATE OF COMPLETION 35

CHRISTIANITY

(Fact or Fiction?)

When the term "Christian" was first used in Antioch (previously known as Seria), around the year 70 AD, it had a completely different meaning than it does today.

> *"And when he had found him, he brought him unto Antioch. And it came to pass, that a whole year they assembled themselves with the church, and taught much people. And the disciples were called Christians first in Antioch."*
> *(Acts 11:26)*

This once-reverently identifying name, which dates back almost two millennia, has now evolved into a mochary in the twenty-first century.

By modern standards, it appears that everyone is a Christian.

Would it surprise you to learn that the term "Christian" was coined by the Roman Empire to signify a clear division between Romans and God's followers and neither God nor God's people actually gave it to us? That's right! The Latin word "Christianus," which means "a follower of Christ," is where the English word "Christian" is derived.

Under the direction of Roman General Titus, the Roman Empire ruled and besieged Jerusalem in the year 70 CE. Much of the city, including the temple, was destroyed during the bloody battle. Their primary language was Latin, & it's from whom the disciples of Jesus were called *"Christians"*.

What then did I mean when I said, "Everyone's a Christian," and "The word "Christian" today doesn't even remotely have the same meaning"?

The answer to this seemingly obvious question is "what makes one a "follower of Christ"," but let's consider it from a biblical perspective first:

1) **We MUST Believe:**
   Being a follower of Christ was never meant to be simple, transitory, or part-time; it isn't based on what we think, what we feel emotionally, or even on our own ideals; rather, it MUST be based on fundamental Christian values, faithfulness, and a commitment to keeping oneself separate from things that are unholy. This is a full-time commitment that should never be taken lightly. We MUST endure (persevere) till the end! (Mark 13:13)

   *"Then Agrippa said unto Paul, Almost thou **persuadest** me to be a Christian." (Acts 26:28)*

   Persuade is defined as:

- cause (someone) to do something through reasoning or argument.
- cause (someone) to believe something, especially after a sustained effort; convince.

Alternatively put, a discipled believer is a True Christian. In order to follow after God, we must deny ourselves, take up our cross, and follow Him (Luke 9:23). It is our obligation. We have made a commitment to do so. It is our duty to bear the cross.

2) We MUST be Discipled:

<u>Disciple</u> is defined as:

- a follower or student of a teacher, leader, or philosopher.
- one who accepts and assists in spreading the doctrines of another

"Then said Jesus to those Jews which believed on him, If ye continue in my word, then are ye my disciples indeed" (John 8:31)

"Beware lest any man spoil you through philosophy and vain deceit, after the tradition of men, after the rudiments of the world, and not after Christ. (Colossians 2:8)

Therefore, the central tenet of being a follower of Jesus is not based on human wisdom but rather on divine wisdom. We must only believe in the scriptures that exclusively derive from God's word if we are to save our souls.

"In the beginning was the Word, and the Word was with God, and the Word was God." (John 1:1)

"And the Word was made flesh, and dwelt among us, (and we Beheld his glory, the glory as of the only begotten of the Father,) full of grace and truth." (John 1:14)

"He that eateth my flesh, and drinketh my blood, dwelleth in me, and I in him." (John 6:56)

"Search the scriptures; for in them ye think ye have eternal life: And they are they which testify of me." (John 5:39)

Because our spiritual home cannot stand without a foundation, discipleship is the very ESSENCE of the Basic Fundamentals of Christian Living.

> *"And are built upon the foundation of the apostles and Prophets, Jesus Christ himself being the chief corner stone; In whom all the building fitly framed together groweth unto an holy temple in the Lord: In whom ye also are builded together for an habitation of God through the Spirit." (Ephesians 2:20-22)*
>
> *"Except the Lord build the house, they labour in vain that build It: except the Lord keep the city, the watchman waketh but in vain." (Psalms 127:1)*

3) We MUST Suffer:

"Yet if any man suffer as a Christian, let him not be ashamed; but let him glorify God on this behalf." (1 Peter 4:16)

"For I will shew him how great things he must suffer for my name's sake." (Acts 9:16)

"Fear none of those things which thou shalt suffer: behold, the devil shall cast some of you into prison, that ye may be tried; and ye shall have tribulation ten days: be thou faithful unto death, and I will give thee a crown of life." (Revelation 2:10)

"And if children, then heirs; heirs of God, and joint-heirs with Christ; if so be that we suffer with him, that we may be also glorified together. For I reckon that the sufferings of this present time are not worthy to be compared with the glory which shall be revealed in us."
(Romans 8:17-18)

"And they departed from the presence of the council, rejoicing that they were counted worthy to suffer shame for his name." (Acts 5:41)

"And labour, working with our own hands: being reviled, we bless; being persecuted, we suffer it: Being defamed, we intreat: we are made as the filth of the world, and are the offscouring of all things unto this day." (1 Corinthians 4:12-13)

Suffering in Christ is a spirit of victory, not of defeat.

"Yea, and all that will live godly in Christ Jesus shall suffer persecution." (2 Timothy 3:12)

"Confirming the souls of the disciples, and exhorting them to continue in the faith, and that we must through much tribulation enter into the kingdom of God." (Acts 14:22)

Suffering reproach, persecution, imprisonment, beatings, and yes even death are considered an honor, and we are to rejoice if/when we find ourselves in these positions. When one's faith is put to the test, their true nature—good or bad—will always come out. The world will be able to tell who we really are serving based on how we handle these trials. (Romans 6:16)

"Ye are our epistle written in our hearts, known and read of all men: Forasmuch as ye are manifestly declared to be the epistle of Christ ministered by us, written not with ink, but with the Spirit of the living God; not in tables of stone, but in fleshy tables of the heart." (2 Corinthians 3:2-3)

4) We MUST Witness:

One of the most effective tools God has given us for inspiring others to follow Christ is witnessing. Through these encounters, we increase our faith, trust, and boldness in the Lord, and as a result, our confidence in Him grows to the point where we actually find ourselves capable of moving mountains.

To effectively witness and lead people to God, I use my spiritual gifts. We can lead folks to the Lord if we use these gifts properly.

There are many ways we can witness, but I have found several to really be effective:

A) **Use your Mouth** - Tell someone what Jesus has done for you!

- Speak evil of no one (James 4:11)
- Share your personal testimony (Acts 10:42)
- Speak kindness (especially to those who hate you)
- Speak wholesome words (1 Peter 3:10)
- Speak life (Acts 5:20)
    - being positive is attractive - like a moth to the flame
    - Life and Death are in the power of the tongue (Prov 18:21)
- Speak truthfully and honestly (1 Peter 2:12)
- Speak good things about people and your church (Luke 6:45)
    - Anointed Preaching
    - Powerful Prayers
    - Impartations of Revelations
    - Gifts of the Spirit

"That the communication of thy faith may become effectual

by the acknowledging of every good thing which is in you in Christ Jesus." (Philemon 6)

B) **<u>Be a light</u>** - Don't hide your light under a bushel (Matthew 5:15)

- Portray the character of Jesus Christ
- How you live you life can either encourage someone to Christ or run them off
- Live your life as a VICTOR not a VICTIM
    - We cannot wave the banner of Victory if we our living a life of defeat
    - Being positively minded produces positive things; being negatively minded produces negative things

What is
THE SIN CYCLE?

Now that we know what to expect as a "Disciple" of Jesus, let's learn HOW to continue on to perfection (Hebrews 6:1) in the construction of our spiritual house through biblical teaching and HOW to become a more effective child of God.

To be completely honest with you, if you would allow me a moment, I would like to share with you the following example of what the Lord revealed to me regarding my previous unhealthy psychological behavior:

The example I'd like to give is of what I'd like to call the dreaded "SIN CYCLE." It is a cycle that constantly repeats itself that prohibits my spirit from being set free.

Note that I DO NOT claim to be a psychologist!
I can only speak from personal experience.

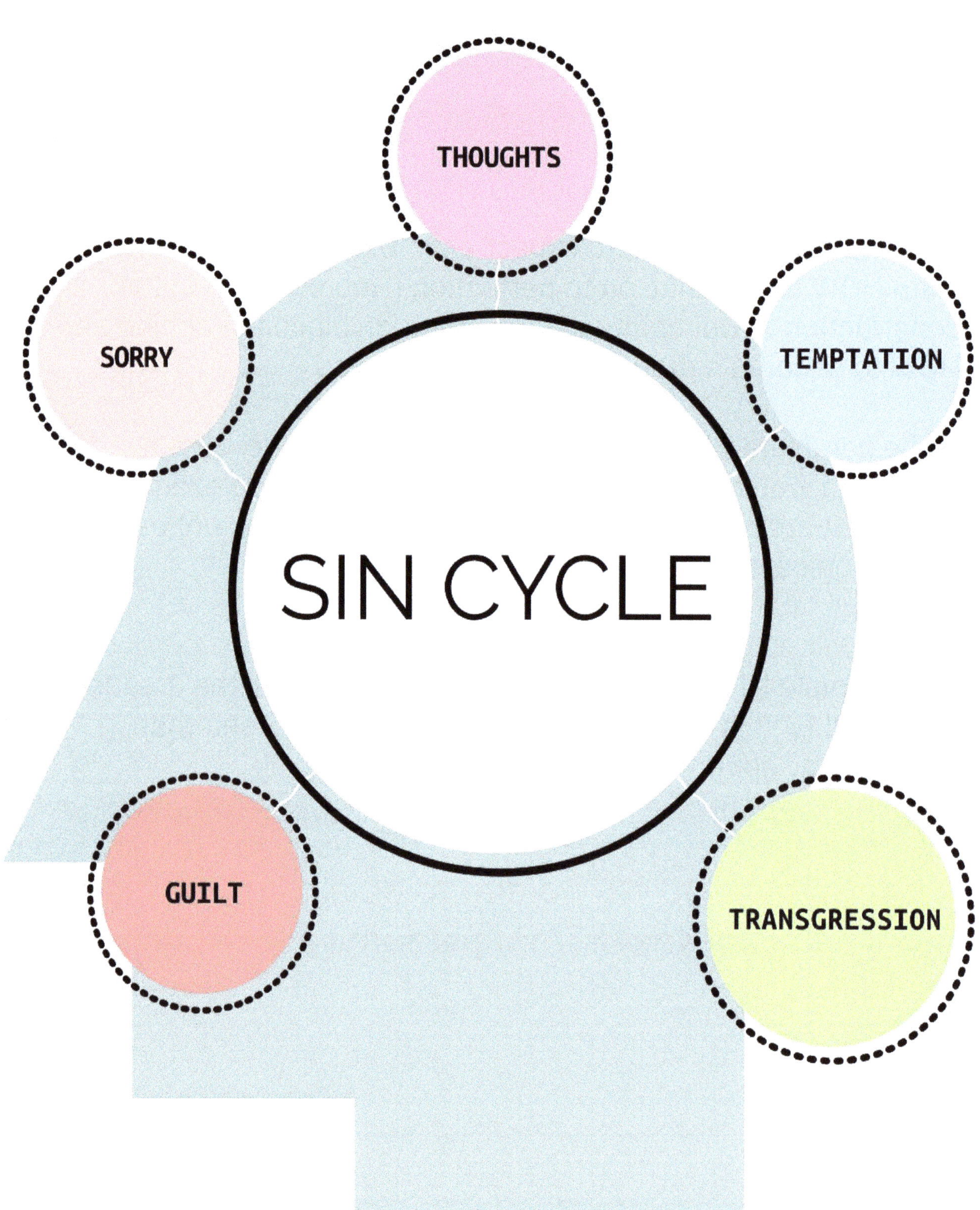
THOUGHTS
SORRY
TEMPTATION
SIN CYCLE
GUILT
TRANSGRESSION

THOUGHTS

2 Cor 4:4 - In whom the god of this world hath blinded the minds of them which believe not, lest the light of the glorious gospel of Christ, who is the image of God, should shine unto them.

2 Cor 11:3 - But I fear, lest by any means, as the serpent beguiled Eve through his subtilty, so your minds should be corrupted from the simplicity that is in Christ.

Eph 4:27 - Neither give place to the devil. (place - opportunity)

Romans 1:28-32 - 28 And even as they did not like to retain God in their knowledge (MINDS), God gave them over to a reprobate MIND, to do those things which are not convenient;

29 Being filled with all unrighteousness, fornication, wickedness, covetousness, maliciousness; full of envy, murder, debate, deceit, malignity; whisperers,

30 Backbiters, haters of God, despiteful, proud, boasters, inventors of evil things, disobedient to parents,

31 Without understanding, covenant-breakers, without natural affection, implacable, unmerciful:

32 Who knowing the judgment of God, that they which commit such things are worthy of death, not only do the same, but have pleasure in them that do them.

Matthew 16:23 - But he turned and said to Peter, "Get behind me, Satan! You are a hindrance[a] to me. For you are not setting your mind on the things of God, but on the things of man."

Rom 12:2 - nd be not conformed to this world: but be ye

transformed by the renewing of your mind, that ye may prove what is that good, and acceptable, and perfect, will of God.

TEMPTATION

1 Cor 10:13 - There hath no temptation taken you but such as is common to man: but God is faithful, who will not suffer you to be tempted above that ye are able; but will with the temptation also make a way to escape, that ye may be able to bear it.

Matthew 26:41 - Watch and pray, that ye enter not into temptation: the spirit indeed is willing, but the flesh is weak.

James 4:7 - Submit yourselves therefore to God. Resist the devil, and he will flee from you.

James 1:12-16 - Blessed is the man who remains steadfast under trial, for when he has stood the test he will receive the crown of life, which God has promised to those who love him. Let no one say when he is tempted, “I am being tempted by God,” for God cannot be tempted with evil, and he himself tempts no one. But each person is tempted when he is lured and enticed by his own desire. Then desire when it has conceived gives birth to sin, and sin when it is fully grown brings forth death. Do not be deceived, my beloved brothers.

Hebrews 2:18 - For because he himself has suffered when tempted, he is able to help those who are being tempted.

Eph 6:11 - Put on the whole armor of God, that you may be able to stand against the schemes of the devil.

TRANSGRESSION

Is 43:25 - I, even I, am he that blotteth out thy transgressions for mine own sake, and will not remember thy sins.

John 8:31-32 - **31** Then said Jesus to those Jews which believed on him, If ye continue in my word, then are ye my disciples indeed;

32 And ye shall know the truth, and the truth shall make you free.

James 1:14 - But each person is tempted when he is lured and enticed by his own desire.

Luke 16:13 - No servant can serve two masters: for either he will hate the one, and love the other; or else he will hold to the one, and despise the other. Ye cannot serve God and mammon.

Gal 6:1 - Brethren, if a man be overtaken in a fault, ye which are spiritual, restore such an one in the spirit of meekness; considering thyself, lest thou also be tempted.

Prov 28:13 - He that covereth his sins shall not prosper: but whoso confesseth and forsaketh them shall have mercy.

GUILT

1 John 2:1 - My little children, these things write I unto you, that ye sin not. And if any man sin, we have an advocate with the Father, Jesus Christ the righteous:

2 Cor 7:10 - For godly sorrow worketh repentance to salvation not to be repented of: but the sorrow of the world worketh death.

Is 6:7 - And he laid it upon my mouth, and said, Lo, this hath touched thy lips; and thine iniquity is taken away, and thy sin purged.

Heb 10:22 - Let us draw near with a true heart in full assurance of faith, having our hearts sprinkled from an evil conscience, and our bodies washed with pure water.

GUILT vs REMORSE

GUILT is NOT regret. Guilt is actually a destructive, emotional & selfish view the enemy uses to create a false sense of change in one's self, whereas REMORSE (godly sorrow) is a selfless, constructive & understanding of one's actions that leads one to a true repentance/conversion.

"Guilt and shame are tools out of the liar and thief's bag. Make sure to not pick them up and use them on yourself or others" - Jeremy Lesley

SORRY

(SORROWFUL or REPENTANCE?)

An apology without change is just manipulation!

2 Cor 7:10 - For godly sorrow worketh repentance to salvation not to be repented of: but the sorrow of the world worketh death.

2 Peter 3:9 - The Lord is not slack concerning his promise, as some men count slackness; but is longsuffering to us-ward, not willing that any should perish, but that all should come to repentance.

Acts 3:19 - Repent ye therefore, and be converted, that your sins may be blotted out, when the times of refreshing shall come from the presence of the Lord.

1 John 1:9 - If we confess our sins, he is faithful and just to forgive us our sins, and to cleanse us from all unrighteousness.

2 Chron 7:14 - If my people, which are called by my name, shall humble themselves, and pray, and seek my face, and turn from their wicked ways; then will I hear from heaven, and will forgive their sin, and will heal their land.

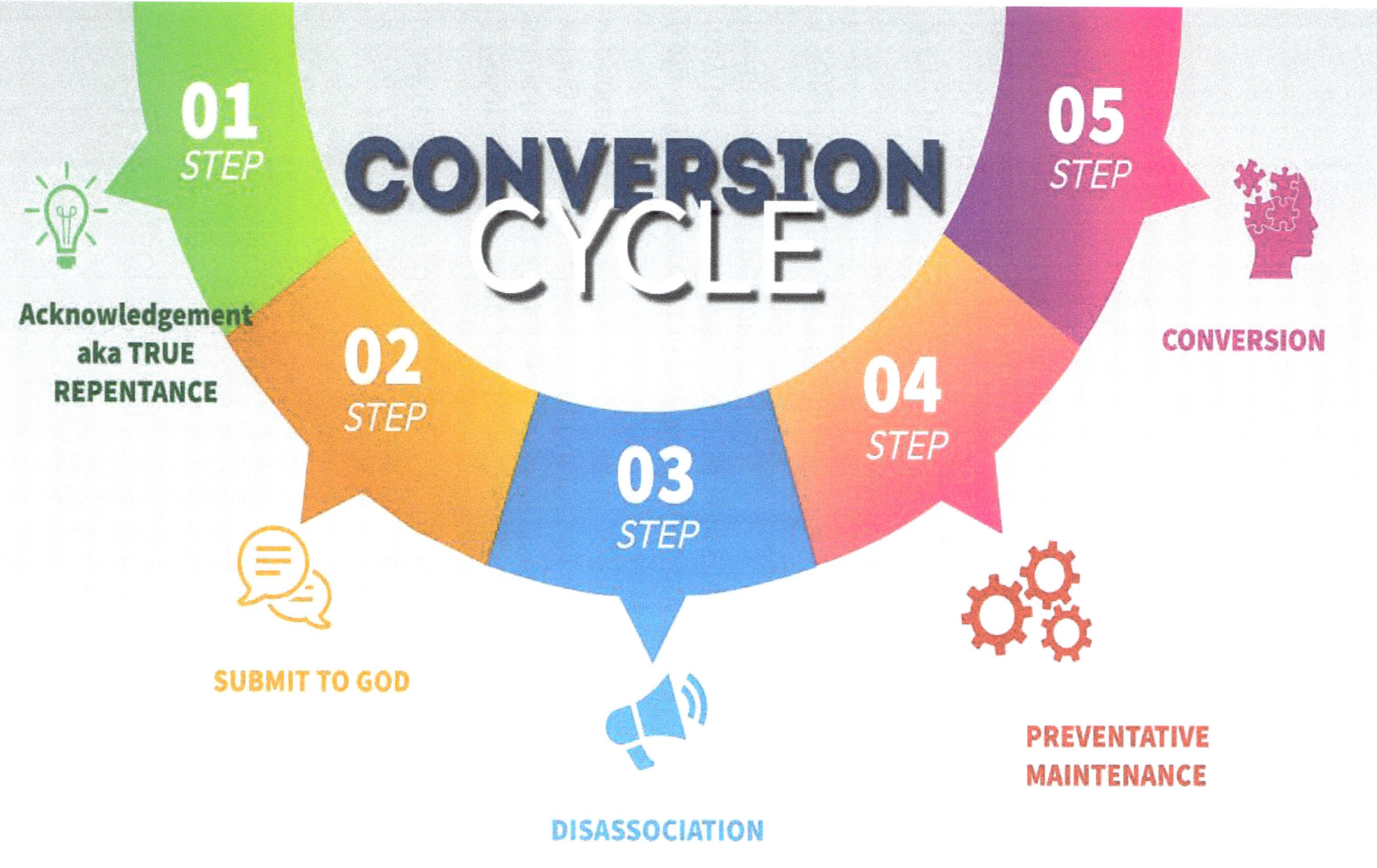
CONVERSION CYCLE
01 STEP
Acknowledgement aka TRUE REPENTANCE
02 STEP
SUBMIT TO GOD
03 STEP
DISASSOCIATION
04 STEP
PREVENTATIVE MAINTENANCE
05 STEP
CONVERSION

ACKNOWLEDGEMENT
(TRUE REPENTANCE)

Psalm 32:5 - I acknowledge my sin unto thee, and mine iniquity have I not hid. I said, I will confess my transgressions unto the Lord; and thou forgavest the iniquity of my sin. Selah.

Psalm 51:3 - For I acknowledge my transgressions: and my sin is ever before me.

Jeremiah 14:20 - We acknowledge, O Lord, our wickedness, and the iniquity of our fathers: for we have sinned against thee.

2 Corinthians 7:9 - Now I rejoice, not that ye were made sorry, but that ye sorrowed to repentance: for ye were made sorry after a godly manner, that ye might receive damage by us in nothing.

SUBMIT TO GOD

(Surrender)

James 4:7 - Submit yourselves therefore to God. Resist the devil, and he will flee from you.

Deuteronomy 11:27-28 - (27)A blessing, if ye obey the commandments of the Lord your God, which I command you this day: (28)And a curse, if ye will not obey the commandments of the Lord your God, but turn aside out of the way which I command you this day, to go after other gods, which ye have not known.

Jeremiah 26:13 - Therefore now amend your ways and your doings, and obey the voice of the Lord your God; and the Lord will repent him of the evil that he hath pronounced against you.

1 Corinthians 15:31 - I protest by your rejoicing which I have in Christ Jesus our Lord, I die daily.

LET GO OF:

- Controlling (others, situations & outcomes)
- Worrying (causes stress, & stress causes:)
    - Disrupted sleep
    - Headaches
    - Difficulty Concentrating
    - Nausea
    - Muscle Tension
    - Chest Pain
    - Exhaustion (lack of motivation)
    - Irritability
    - Abdominal Pain
    - Lightheadedness & Dizziness
    - Elevated levels of the stress hormone, Cortisol
    - 85% of all sickness is STRESS RELATED
- Money Issues (you cannot solve money issues with money)
- Relationships Problems
    - Oftentimes, people bottle up or keep their stress to themselves, which makes it difficult for their partners to understand what they are going through and to provide support. Not

    - dealing with stress can create a negative cycle where partners “catch” each other's stress.

- Future (Hypothetical Things - roleplaying in our minds)

DISASSOCIATION

(Flee)

1 Corinthians 6:18 - Flee fornication. Every sin that a man doeth is without the body; but he that committeth fornication sinneth against his own body.

2 Timothy 2:22 - Flee also youthful lusts: but follow righteousness, faith, charity, peace, with them that call on the Lord out of a pure heart.

As newly born-again Christians, one of the best things we can do is establish new, healthy habits. It might be necessary for you to make some new friends who will lift you up rather than bring you down to accomplish this.

If you have been born-again, you now belong to a new family of church members who ought to support, edify, and comfort one another.

Every shepherd in the Kingdom of God should exhort his flock to spend one night in intercessory prayer. The flock will grow stronger as a result of this.

2 Corinthians 6:14 - Be ye not unequally yoked together with unbelievers: for what fellowship hath righteousness with unrighteousness? and what communion hath light with darkness?

PREVENTATIVE MEASURE

(Steps taken to prevent an unplanned mishap)
Law & Order of Reaping & Sowing

Philippians 2:1-8 - If there be therefore any consolation in Christ, if any comfort of love, if any fellowship of the Spirit, if any bowels and mercies,

2 Fulfil ye my joy, that ye be likeminded, having the same love, being of one accord, of one mind.

3 Let nothing be done through strife or vainglory; but in lowliness of mind let each esteem other better than themselves.

4 Look not every man on his own things, but every man also on the things of others.

5 Let this mind be in you, which was also in Christ Jesus:

6 Who, being in the form of God, thought it not robbery to be equal with God:

7 But made himself of no reputation, and took upon him the form of a servant, and was made in the likeness of men:

8 And being found in fashion as a man, he humbled himself, and became obedient unto death, even the death of the cross.

Philippians 3:15 - Let us therefore, as many as be perfect, be thus minded: and if in any thing ye be otherwise minded, God shall reveal even this unto you.

We are planting for the coming harvest!

A wonderful way to change our minds into Christ's is through prayer and fasting.

Isaiah 58:6-8 - Is not this the fast that I have chosen? to loose the bands of wickedness, to undo the heavy burdens, and to let the oppressed go free, and that ye break every yoke?

7 Is it not to deal thy bread to the hungry, and that thou bring the poor that are cast out to thy house? when thou seest the naked, that thou cover him; and that thou hide not thyself from thine own flesh?

8 Then shall thy light break forth as the morning, and thine health shall spring forth speedily: and thy righteousness shall go before thee; the glory of the Lord shall be thy reward.

God's Spirit endowed us with supernatural power when He filled us with His Spirit. We are given the ability and authority to carry out what Jesus accomplished through the Holy Spirit.

Avoiding worldly practices will undoubtedly keep our faith strong in the Lord.

Romans 6:16 - Know ye not, that to whom ye yield yourselves servants to obey, his servants ye are to whom ye obey; whether of sin unto death, or of obedience unto righteousness?

Matthew 6:24 - No man can serve two masters: for either he will hate the one, and love the other; or else he will hold to the one, and despise the other. Ye cannot serve God and mammon.

Galatians 6:7-9 - Be not deceived; God is not mocked: for whatsoever a man soweth, that shall he also reap.

8 For he that soweth to his flesh shall of the flesh reap corruption; but he that soweth to the Spirit shall of the Spirit reap life everlasting.

9 And let us not be weary in well doing: for in due season we shall reap, if we faint not.

CONVERSION

(Turn Around - Transform - Change)

Spiritual Maturity

<u>**2 Corinthians 5:17**</u> – Therefore if any man be in Christ, he is a new creature: old things are passed away; behold, all things are become new.

<u>**Ezekiel 36:26**</u> – A new heart also will I give you, and a new spirit will I put within you: and I will take away the stony heart out of your flesh, and I will give you an heart of flesh.

<u>**Romans 12:2**</u> – And be not conformed to this world: but be ye transformed by the renewing of your mind, that ye may prove what is that good, and acceptable, and perfect, will of God.

<u>**Luke 6:43-45**</u> – For a good tree bringeth not forth corrupt fruit; neither doth a corrupt tree bring forth good fruit.

44 For every tree is known by his own fruit. For of thorns men do not gather figs, nor of a bramble bush gather they grapes.

45 A good man out of the good treasure of his heart bringeth forth that which is good; and an evil man out of the evil treasure of his heart bringeth forth that which is evil: for of the abundance of the heart his mouth speaketh.

<u>**Jeremiah 32:38-40**</u> – And they shall be my people, and I will be their God:

39 And I will give them one heart, and one way, that they may fear me for ever, for the good of them, and of their children after them:

40 And I will make an everlasting covenant with them, that I will not turn away from them, to do them good; but I will put my fear in their hearts, that they shall not depart from me.

Psalm 119:11 - Thy word have I hid in mine heart, that I might not sin against thee.

Certificate of Completion

UNDERSTANDING CONVERSION

THIS CERTIFICATE IS PROUDLY PRESENTED TO

____

I personally would like to congratulate you on successfully completing the UNDERSTANDING CONVERSION course. I sincerely hope and pray that the knowledge you gain from taking this course will help you to continue to walk faithfully with the Lord Jesus Christ.

______________________ SIGNATURE

______________________ DATE

www.ingramcontent.com/pod-product-compliance
Ingram Content Group UK Ltd.
Pitfield, Milton Keynes, MK11 3LW, UK
UKHW050142280726
14058UKWH00006B/784

9 781387 548576